In a Field of Hallowed Be

Also by Timothy Geiger

Blue Light Factory
The Curse of Pheromones
Weatherbox

Chapbooks
Holler
Radium
Cathedral
Four Windows
Migratory Patterns
Small Passages
Einstein and the Ants
Another Atmosphere
Catechism Days
Proving the Light

In a Field of Hallowed Be

Timothy Geiger

Terrapin Books

© 2024 by Timothy Geiger
Printed in the United States of America.
All rights reserved.
No part of this book may be reproduced in any manner, except for brief quotations embodied in critical articles or reviews.

Terrapin Books
4 Midvale Avenue
West Caldwell, NJ 07006

www.terrapinbooks.com

ISBN: 978-1-947896-77-2
Library of Congress Control Number: 2024940223

First Edition

Cover art by Ashley Geiger
Beekeeper
Digital collage

Cover design by Diane Lockward

For Ashley,
who got me to here

Contents

After All	3

I

Overcast	9
No Bee Balm	10
Weather Report	12
Animals in the Dark	13
Binomial	15
Night Lights	17
Azaleas	19

Orbits	25
Back Country	27
Smoke	29
The Lost World	31
Blanket	33
Legacy	36

II

Certainty	39
Maybe Mice	40
Invisible Birds	41
Thanksgiving	43
Retreat	45
Winter Follows	46
If a Tree Falls	47

Stump	51
The Hidden Spring	54
Drift	56
Grackle, Grackle	57
Maybe the Jay	58

Take Flight	60
Hex	61
Consoling the Flock	63

III

Limestone	67
Condolence	68
Father at the End	70
Pretense	72
Passion	74
Country Dark	76
The Five Hearts of Texas	77
Desperados	83
Xiuhtecuhtli	84

A Decent God	87
The Penitent	89
Guardian of the Farm	90
Field Guide	91
Hollow	97
Ending	98
The Center	100
Acknowledgments	105
About the Author	107

the field tells none of its turned story
it lies under its low cloud like a waiting river

—W. S. Merwin

After All

I carry my impermanence in layers of bone,
muscle, skin, this blue t-shirt and jeans,
out here, to this permanence
that even now may be fading.
Here is my land, a house, a barn, five acres,
some chickens, and goats.
                          The field reaches
to the tree line, full of ticks and timothy grass,
and listens intently when I tell it that
one day I will make it an orchard of apple and cherry.
I will keep it mowed, watered, and cared for
as it's never been cared for before.
It's just earth,
             and clay down to the frost line
and who knows how much farther
till the limestone appears, makes a backbone
it all balances on. But up here, as we say,
in the country, it's just field.
                             It's the place
I never thought I'd arrive at after that alley
off South Street, nineteen and too stoned
to find my way back to the apartment's address
my friend Ron gave me only an hour before.
Before what?
            Before we snorted six more lines
in the bathroom of Jim's Steaks, and he left
with a guy nicknamed Evil to score two more
eight balls of crank. He won't be home in the morning,
or for another three days, and I'll be gone by then,

catching the bus back up Market Street, then
west to Bryn Mawr.
      But first, I need to make my way
back to his place, I need to have an argument
with the traffic light, the homeless guy with no hands,
the Hari Krishna in a robe so orange it burns my eyes.
I need to stare down the stares of every passerby
on that city street,
     the shame I felt surrounded
by families, tourists from Brazil, the cops
who'll stop and ask from the backs of their horses,
"What's wrong with your eyes?" I tell them,
I was born this way,
      always looking sideways, or down…
Eventually, I'll make it to his doorstep,
to the bus terminal, to Bryn Mawr where I'll hitch
a ride with my Uncle who's been drinking since lunch,
since he broke his spine online at the plant,
back to my parent's house and classes the next day—
a handful of core requirements at the local
two-year college—still having no idea where I'm going,
or what
    I'm supposed to do with my life.
I'll find the words to tell my mother,
*Yes, I'm fine, I was shopping, just shopping,
that's all,* skipping stairs on my way to my room
and a blessed sleep I haven't had for days.
My heart will finally slow down, the walls will stop
dissolving, and I'll say, *Enough,*
      and find my way
here, 35 years from there. Does what happened
in between finally make any difference, what little
I remember of it at least, which is less and less

the older I become?
          There were places I found myself
I should never have been—the junkie's squat,
the police lineup, passed out in the backseat
of my alcoholic uncle's car—but also places where
I always felt I was meant to be.
          And really,
most of those were like here, their own particular
shades of green, essential to the overall compositions
of forest and meadow and mountain burning off
into the clouds.
          Alabama, Minnesota, Montana to
Ohio, March through October the maples erupting
in emerald jackets, peaking a different orange,
then fallen and raked to a different burning,
rising into the night sky and drifting always east,
covering all the nameless constellations
until the morning rose.
          And each journey to get here,
miles under the same tired sky revolving over
the same earth that never went anywhere after all.
And the memories of them—
          of Ron, dead at 27
from hepatitis, of Evil, who I never met but who
got gunned down the following week, of my Uncle,
who finally quit drinking then died within a month,
of my mother gone 10 years, who listened
and didn't believe a word I said—
          all gone, but each
got me to here, where my bones stretch against the skin
of my fingertips plunging into this clay, as kildeer rise
like ghosts from the milkweed of the west pasture,
where I am asking this field to show me how to live.

Overcast

—for Dean Young

There are so many dead baby rabbits in the yard
I have given up hope. The powerlines buzzing
like a broken doorbell above the cornfield next door.
The dog found the nest hidden in the garden
and dragged them out, one by one. Four pine trees
shuffled their backs turning. He didn't kill them
right away, but his roughhousing was their sundering.
I'm trying hard not to redefine play as murder.
He carried each almost gently, like you might carry
someone else's used handkerchief. A plastic grocery sack
waved alms from the field fence. He left one beneath
the crab apple, another abandoned by the garden shed,
one in the middle of the path, leading back
to the chicken coop. Two days later I'm still finding
their swollen gray fur bodies blossoming flies
above the uncut lawn. The toes on a baby bunny's foot
are delicate whispers. There are graves and then
there are more graves. He didn't know they would die
so easy, so maybe he too has lost hope. It's hard
not to feel like the whole world is ending, easier
to forgive him, easier still to feel sorry, the weather
in the yard cajoling the clouds to come down to earth.

No Bee Balm

Honeybee burst
    from the tongues
of pink petals
    a tulip's mouth
golden grains
    of pollen trailing
from his cheeks
    he combs a leg
sensual as water
    on a Jamaica beach
where you texted
    wish you were here
as I checked the hive
    the brood racks
bare of honey
    and everything
is all right
    when clouds
begin to swarm
    from the north
and the slums
    of Kingston
where you painted
    a school yesterday
have grown
    thinner hats of tin
roofs and gutters
    draining into
already drowned streets
    pushing boundaries

the queen
>   sends out
another scattershot
>   of drones
to surface and skim
>   the apple blossoms
drop skittering
>   like snow flakes
into mud
>   and the graves
keep multiplying
>   *the cemeteries*
spread like water
>   you said as another
April snow
>   shower another
pile of dead bees
>   below the hive
entrance another
>   honeybee burst
in the cold

Weather Report

I like the days hot
though it's a matter of context.
Tracy blames the moon,
says it pulls the waves
which pull the clouds,
the wisp and vapor that make
this heat. Like the planet is just
a clockwork mechanism
generating degrees,
stuck and throttling ever up.
Stifling, like the inside
of the shoulder length rubber glove
she sticks in the cow's back end
up to her elbow. The heifer
rolls her eyes and bellows.
"There's nothing here," she says,
wiping her bangs back
with a shoulder, "not anymore."
My palm rests between the cow's eyes,
fingers tapping.
After lunch, I'll walk the west pasture
for the sorry remains
of what will be her third
miscarriage. I'll remember
to bring a shovel this time,
setting out under the blazing
midday sun. This heat
barren as the day began.

Animals in the Dark

There is no solace in what I want
anymore. I conjure the moonless field
from the odor of milkweed and alfalfa,
morning frost the only shimmering
I set foot into. Of course, I know my way.
Day after day, I rise in this dark,
dress and go out to feed the animals—
the goats, chickens, ducks, and pigs
that share this farm. Sometimes
the wind burns my cheeks, an estuary
of desire and misdirection all around.
I feel my age in the rush at my temples,
each five-gallon bucket of water
groans when I stand. By now, my spine
despises everything about me,
but there is no turning back.
Has everything always been moving
to here, this patch of land in the country,
or just away from the city lights,
cars angry at one another over nothing
more than space, prowlers hiding behind
their parked shadows, house cats
left out to slaughter birds? Thirty acres
across the corn stubble to my east
the neighbor's lights flicker on. I hear
but don't see the dog at the fence line
chasing a rabbit or field mouse back
into the underbrush, so I keep moving
till I'm opening the barn door. This
is exactly what I wanted—surrounded

by hungry mouths, a waking din
of perplexed, demanding noises.
Pressing into the back of my legs,
pleading underfoot, pulling me down
till I too am buried in the rough hay
that serves as their nightly beds.
After sunrise, they will all go to pasture
with full bellies and muddy snouts,
beaks that poke and turn the wet clay
for stray slugs or snails, but for now,
in the easy dark that surrounds
and embraces us, they devour me.

Binomial

>*—a mathematical expression consisting of two terms connected by a plus sign or a minus sign.*
>   —Merriam-Webster

Two horses grazed apart,
one on each side of the corral
split in half by a stockade fence
stretching up and disappearing
over the grassy hill. The chestnut
watched the dappled gray, more
gaze than graze in her stance.
It may have gone on forever,
not the fence receding, but
the longing the horses felt
to be near one another,
the same ache I still feel
when I miss my mother's voice.
It's easy to forget it's not my job
to put the world back together.
Six hours and an axe, I could
probably take that fence down,
split and cast the cedar rails,
just fence post stumps
sticking up from the ground.
Two weeks before she died
I asked her why she wanted
her ashes in an urn behind
a granite slab. She told me
she'd always lived too far away
to be scattered in some ocean
so it all became about remaining

whole. There is no ocean, no lake,
or even a river for miles around
here—just a pasture beyond
the corral, beyond the fence line
stretching to the sunrise,
mirages in the blurred distance
of perspective, into which
the separate horses now run.

Night Lights

Like a child lighting prayer candles
after Sunday mass,
sunk in mysteries of incense
smoke and faith, tonight
I'm full of other illuminations,
a new world waking in the dark.

After the flicker into animation
of the television screen
I turn to the aquarium's steady blue
sputter before rising
to clean up the white emanations
spilling from the open refrigerator door.

I pass the dog rattling her tags,
chasing endless rabbits in her sleep.
Then, the thump and patter
of the cat where she doesn't belong,
eyes like glass reflecting candles,
specter of two open windows.

Outside to the back porch
where I imagine heaven
as the center of the constellations,
whirling a pattern of perpetual light
when I spin around fast
in the swiveling deck chair.

When I stop, they become pinpricks again,
tiny holes in the black

curtains of dark matter
closing back in on themselves.
Once again, I'm stalled
before something wonderful glowing.

Azaleas

First Holy Communion
and Nixon caught lying—
both on the same day.
I wasn't old enough
to understand why
either of them mattered,
but I'm in my best suit
just home from church
where the Latin phrases
were adrift like spices—
cinnamon, nutmeg,
frankincense, thyme,
sancta mater Dei
filling the perfumed air.
The pews were packed
with grandparents, uncles,
aunts and distant cousins,
and Sister Catherine,
my catechism teacher,
a shadow who spoke
to no one and vanished
out the side door
before I even got
to transubstantiation.
Back home, my father
is yelling at the TV,
"stinking crook," and
"lying sack of crap,"
as guests are arriving
to celebrate me,

my grandmother stationed
in the small foyer, jaw
agape at my father,
trying not to drop
the Rum cake she spent
all last night baking.
Needing out, after
my whole morning spent
in the confines of God,
I sneak behind her
through the front door
and into the bushes
with a handful of marbles
and a homemade slingshot,
stooped in the space
behind the azaleas
and the front steps where
I think no one can see.
But I'm not interested
in dropping doves
or robins from the air,
or plunking a starburst
in a car's windshield.
I just wanted to watch
everyone arriving, carrying
presents like new clothes,
picture books and cards
full of more money
I'd have nowhere to spend.
I crouched in the dirt
watching the bees visit
the pink and white flowers—
almost like their own

communion—I thought,
but knew I was missing
something, their wings
tracing hymns through
the otherwise somber air.
I could hear my mother
through the front window
telling my father to shut
off the TV, my father
insisting there were
more important things
happening, until
it became an argument
about what mattered most—
this monumental day
I entered the age of reason,
the body and blood
I'd been given for it—
and my father's silence
lost by default.
That's when I heard him
come out the front door
and call my name
up and down the block.
And as I rose from behind
the azaleas, shirt untucked,
clip-on tie undone,
my father shook his head
and said I'd better not
let my mother catch me.
He ran a rough hand
through my hair, snapped
my tie back in place,

and told me to stand
in front of the azaleas
to look reverent and
promise him never to lie.
My father started taking
pictures, the battered
Nikon in his hands,
April sun at his back,
lost behind the lens
trying to capture time.
He'd given up on politics
and everything else
that had to do with the day,
telling me to smile, but
not like that, "You don't
want to look like a monkey."
When I look closely
at those photographs,
the infinite background
of consecrated pink
and purely white blossoms,
I can still see the mud stains
on my praying hands
and ground into my knees.

Orbits

Dust motes in the morning
        light beaming beneath
    the bedroom window shade
and a dream of Mr._____
        (what was his name?)
    my seventh-grade science teacher
already shaking with the ALS
        that would kill him
    two years after he said,
"Everything either orbits
        or moves in waves." He loved
    to talk about Kepler,
and Tycho Brahe who lost
        his nose in a duel, and of course
    Galileo, who suffered
for the sins of proof. The walls
        of his classroom draped black
    with star charts, when the lights
turned out, they glowed
        like dying sparks.
    Hanging from the ceiling tiles
a replica solar system—
        spray-painted Styrofoam balls—
    demonstrated eclipses and apogees.
One day before third period
        we watched the space shuttle
    disintegrate on a TV set
somewhere over Dallas, Texas,
        then we watched him cry.
    Inconsolable. I'd forgotten that

till this morning when the dust
        proved his point,
    namelessly carrying me halfway
to where I never expected to go.

Back Country

Out here, it's easy to fall in love
with it all, green pasture sprawl
to bluestem meadow to poplar forest,
each superseding the endless miles.
The hilly road bends and collides
into the blinding sun's glare.
Just as easy to stop paying attention,
crash and die at a too-sharp turn.

It's like Bobby Joe Buckwalter
all over again. *BJ* we called him
in the sixth grade, his nostrils
flared in a slick runny mess, his whole
face pocked with angry pink sores.
I remember him whenever I drive
on winding roads like these. Probably,
because his name makes me think
of getting lost in the back country.

And how he always wanted to trade
his bruised apple or slimy plum
for my star-sprinkled donuts,
Ho Ho's, and chocolate Tastykakes.
And when I'd tell him to get bent,
he'd spit on my sweets and take them
anyway. He was much bigger than me.

Like this eighteen-wheeler creeping
up my tail now. Where in the hell
did he come from? And where

could he be going, miles from any
interstate, on this winding country
road? His mother was a whore,
but I didn't know it then. Not until
the morning my oldest sister read
in the local paper's crime log—
BJ's mom got busted for indecency.

Back then I was too young to know
what indecency was. BJ died
that summer, from a bee sting
of all the crazy things. Turns out
there wasn't much he wasn't
allergic to, which explained
the sores that covered his cheeks,
the wadded-up snotty tissues he left
in little piles wherever he sat.

When I look back now, that big truck
behind me is gone, and there was
no turnoff I ever saw. Appearing
and disappearing, BJ taught me
to appreciate what my lunch bag held
any given day. Whatever comes
between now and the next blind turn,
the road narrows at the bridge,
the creek below keeps rushing by.

Smoke

Honest to God, I used to know a guy named Vinny Christ
who'd call me every Saturday night. Without identifying himself,
and without regard for the voice on the other end of the line,
he'd growl, "Hey man, you got any smoke?"
                                            Often
it was one of my roommates who answered the phone
and passed the question off to me. "Vinny's jonezin' again,"
he'd mumble above the lip of the bong's polished edge.

Those college nights, what we looked for was what we thought
might postpone the inevitable confrontation with our lives.
Because I knew someone, who knew someone, I usually had
something, but never enough to share with Vinny.
                                                With him
everything was green: *Did you know the Constitution was written
on weed? That Jefferson and Washington grew pot on their farms.
Which is why hemp is considered the most versatile textile…*
                                                     whatever
the heck that meant. Illicit highs, expanded consciousness,
curled up in a perfumed ball on the couch, listening
to the buzz and grind of eighties college radio, the electric fade
of molecules breaking down, lungs absorbing…
                                                 Whatever.
We just wanted to waste time watching light change direction.
By the following morning, I pled guilty out of pity
and overcharged Vinny for something mixed with oregano.

Funny, the last I knew he was a delivery boy for a pharmacy—
each morning a tiny blue sun dissolving on his tongue—
took up popping when he couldn't get reefer, months after

I graduated, packed my things, and moved away.
                                        What little
I remember of those eternal Saturday nights—doled out in
cellophane proportions, becoming fire then dissipating as smoke—
so much light refracting off the polished edge, the warm inhaled kiss.

The Lost World

Back in my day, when the world
broke you stopped and got off,
put the chain back on the derailleur,
or later, popped the hood and wiggled
your finger on the idle. Any kid
could look at something or other
and understand it— *who needed
instructions anyway?* But then
they made it all so complicated—
the trusty carburetor found itself
replaced by the fuel injector,
the zipper's metal teeth crimped
into Velcro's plastic hooks,
fire became the microwave's purview,
and every page in every library
began converting to binary (which
you have to keep reminding yourself
means ones and zeroes.)
So much raw data backed up
on chips and whirling titanium disks:
all music, this month's video
of the new Madonna on TV, the stories
on the evening news, most poetry,
and every single snapshot
you trusted your life had been—
click, the baptism, *click,* graduation,
click, the wedding, *pop,* power failure—
all the files you forgot to save
on a flickering, then dead, black screen.
No wonder you're always dreading

the coming shift of the poles,
an electromagnetic pulse to wipe us
straight back to the Stone Age.
Till then, you'll just continue
clicking away like nothing is wrong,
animating the backgrounds
and digitizing the sources.
It's all you can do to reminisce—
those were the days (when having
a kickstand made all the difference)—
realizing that animated kid, now
weightless against the green screen,
was you, and even though you can't
hold him anymore, it doesn't mean
you should ever let him go.

Blanket

This is the voice
that whispers like sleet
every insomniac night
to a dead mother's ear.
She's not here, she'll never be
anywhere again
in range of these words,
this rearview childhood
receding from view—

the starburst nightlight
by the door,
the blanket folded
at the foot of the bed
speckled with yellow ducks
wearing red boots,
sailboats stabilized
in a field of blue,

a cracked jar of nickels
under the bottom bunk,
drawers full of AWOL
plastic green army men,
and an audience of stuffed animals
lining the bedroom shelf—
youngest of seven
staying behind when
everyone moved away for good.

***

Now, brothers and sisters
carry miles
across state lines, static
phone calls once a year,
infrequent visits
for weddings, a baptism—
occasional entries
and curt exits from
and into each other's lives.

Indifferent cities exhale,
and older brothers
are cast to another day.
Stones on office chair
cushions, sunk
and conforming
to the shapes of backsides
widening every month.

Sisters take little ones
on field trips through
the museum of daily
catastrophes, then hunch
by the coffee maker
watching the slow drip,
waiting for a call
from anywhere else
to come.

  ***

This is the voice
on the other end

of that anywhere else,
thinking it just needs
to quiet and listen,
thinking the past
is a miserly god
doling out pinches
of reclamation like sugar.

It wants to cash in
every dull nickel—
every missing button
of furry blind eyes
watching countless battles
from bedroom shelves—
to feel, one more time,
the blanket

stretch long enough
to cover our bare toes,
keep December at bay,
wrap all our bodies
into one shape,
one family adrift
on the king-size bed
colliding with the endless
ocean of sleep.

Legacy

—after a line from Oscar Gonzales

I've cast aside the grieving songs
      carried my father's body as far as I can
      into the field where the goldenrods rise
I've balanced the clouds crooked on their stands
      set the bones of the broken wren's wing
      these catechisms dissolving in my hands
I've bent before the cross contrite
      watched the vinegar turn to sand
      the wheel spoke rattled wild and broke
I've sunk black stones into this land
      scratched the names in time's dull bark
      a harvest lost to winter remands
I've tried to forget the hero's tale
      murdered the child who rose a man

II

Certainty

Something calls from the holler,
calls again in the brushed silence
of sun-glossed autumn leaves.
Almost a shrieking, not quite
a caw or scream, sound of metal
tearing, vocalized and spit back
through a beak's hollow portent,
so it must be a bird of sorts.
But the spot of a red-tailed hawk
circling just below the cloud mist
is too high up, too certain
in its fixed circumference of sky
to have possibly made the call.
Perhaps the sound, the shrieking,
was meant to summon the one
above—a mate calling, or neighbor
warning, *This space in the holler
is occupied.* As if in answer,
a train whistle lows, borrowing
distance. The steady rumble
of the rail's steel wheelsets
is another destination to reach
mile after mile away. Another
ending that cannot be heard—
the holler stills, the call goes
silent, everything imperceptible
waits for the coming cold.

Maybe Mice

Between the oak paneled ceiling
and the rusted steel roof
the mice have built a republic
in the insulation batts,
burrows and tunnels winding
throughout the fiberglass.
Velvet brown and midnight,
clouds for bellies, they skitter,
dig, and occasionally squeak
from one side of the cabin
to the other. What I can't see
I imagine, and so I've invented
mice. Not squirrels, or raccoons,
or chipmunks, or (God forbid) rats,
but the tiny presence and collusion
of flat black eyes, whiskers finer
than corn silk, tiny paws pattering
their way unchallenged
through the dark. I imagine
a whole new city unfolding,
the architecture unparalleled,
above the oak paneled ceiling.
I remain a tourist below.

Invisible Birds

I have not seen a single bird, though I hear them—
their *cheeps* and *squeaks* and *twee-twees*—from inside
this tiny cabin built into the hill of the holler
where I've bundled myself against the steel-cold wind
four hundred and fifty miles from my family.
Out one of five windows, my eyes scan the valley
looking for them. But they keep hidden in the swirl
of red and gold leaves that is the tree cover
overhead. I say overhead, but it is really all around.
Their calls descend and surround the chill stillness
that drapes the air.

          On our daily phone call, my son
laments a life lost to the zombies on his computer.
He shoots twice and dodges but can't seem to get
beyond their grasp. The static voices he talks to and
plays with, and that I can hear in the background,
are also hundreds of miles away—friends he's never seen
but hopes to meet one day. He tells me of their plans
for a trip to Alabama where they all hope to meet up
next summer. Talks about driving, then getting a flight
when he realizes it's too far for a sixteen-year-old
on his own.

          I think back to beige waiting room walls,
black and white prints of seabirds staggered on them,
and my then nine-year-old son with a puzzle on the floor
beneath a poster of a red giraffe asking, *Just how tall
do you think I am,* just before we learned the letters
ADHD. "Mild really," the doctor said, "his whirling gears
overstimulated, trying to do too much at once."
And how this led to his shyness of the world,

introversion, anxiety disorder, Ritalin, methamphetamine,
simply put, why he was labeled "weird" by everyone
at school.

      But since then, he's embraced that word—
keeps quiet, mostly to himself, scouting his way
through the tangle of schoolyard bullies,
slogging to the car and the short drive home.
After homework, a snack, and after decompression,
he plants himself in his bedroom, bathed
in the blue light of a computer screen, leveling up
by shooting zombies, talking nonsense to the voices
that call themselves Devil Dog and Stick2002. They joke,
prod, and cajole him towards something that sounds
like happiness.

          I have never seen the faces that belong
to those voices (I don't even know their real names),
and I still have not seen a single bird. I can only
imagine their wings, the shadow of a plumage
that navigates the air above, when I hear them
from this cabin over four hundred miles from my son.
When I hang up after tonight's call, after he's paused
his game, those voices on his end and these birds
on mine will listen, unseen and somehow all around,
after he's told me as he always does, *It's all ok, Dad,
my day was fine.*

Thanksgiving

Down in the holler
the orange car rusts,
bones of a steel spine
drop below the chassis.
At the path's end,
a scattered pile
of treated lumber,
arsenic leeches
into the underbrush,
and a discarded coil
of black irrigation tube
making a ring around
two gray squirrels
digging for seeds.
        Long ago
something pushed
the ground to a jagged ridge
rising from the valley.
Tectonic activity,
shifting stone plates,
bubbling up to break
the surface.
        Now the path
deliberately erodes
each steady rain—red clay
scratches old scabs
in the gravel trails—
the ground collects chaff
we leave behind.
The gray squirrels

gather their portion,
discontent beneath
the November sky
overcasting the morning,
rubble and debris
all around.

Retreat

After the first light
snow dissolves
in the morning sun,
the fog appears ghostlike—
spirit of all the fallen
stick and leaf scatter
across the forest floor.
Sunrise and I'm cold
of heart, bruised
as the apple dropped
from the countertop—
these words becoming
snow, thawing
in the sun.   This solitude,
self-imposed, away from
everyone, away from
faces that fill my days,
like fallen sticks and leaves
in another forest
of work and obligation.
I remain detached here
as the temperature
rises and the wind
wreaks a little havoc
in my hair. Icicles daring
the roofline's gutter
melt back to rain.

Winter Follows

—after TuFu

when it comes (and it always comes)
in the swift river offering
and taking away
           all floating
yellow pointed elm leaf

elbow of willow stick drowned
caps of black walnut seed

ditch litter's autumn edge
      golden and leaning
into November's arms

         another great dispersal

bluegill husk autopsied
      under hours gone weary
from lack-of-sun days

this half-forgotten year
of triumph and grief

is a trail of bootsteps
back up
      the mud-worn path
and into the bygone world
where I was weeping when it began

If a Tree Falls

Oak leaves like sails, billowing then pulled taut—
November wind makes the black rotted trunk
contract then expand like a labored breath,
the roots grab deep, darker soil—the whole tree
an uncarved mizzen in this winter storm.
But eyes can't perceive what's below the bark,
as an icy mist rips in like God's sneeze,
dead leaves spinning in a gyre, scattered
across snow's unraveling tablecloth.
Not the cold assaults on the senses, which
can be seen and heard and felt, but the signs
and portents that foretell their happening—
the stillness of snow after wind exhales
the stark repercussions of what comes next.

Stump

Oh what
        must have
                been and
where did
        the body
                go?
Limbs
        chainsawed
                stacked
to hearth
        cast ironed
                heat
trunk sawn
        to board
                and stud.
Banner
        and flag
                of scatter
leaf shake
        surrendered
                to dirt.
How long
        ago?
                So long
this stretch
        scratched
                a sky
neck craned
        look up.

                        Oh conifer
fragrance
            lingering
                        long after
the body
            goes.
                        This body
trying
            to collect
                        so much
past tense.
            What's lost
                        is lost
and trying
            to get
                        it back
makes time
            stop
                        makes less
room to
            remember
                        space
is limited.
            So things
                        fall down
to ash
            sawdust
                        and rot
to field
            loam.
                        The past
another

    buried

        box

roots

     unplumbed

        underground.

The Hidden Spring

11/24/17	11/24/19

We were just starting out.

    I'd been hiking all day.

A frozen November
wedding outside.

    They told me to look for the spring
    in the holler by the shooting range.

You wore a rabbit fur coat.

    I saw nothing in the cold there.

Christmas lights burned
all around the castle.

    The timothy grass,
    dried and shorn, snapped
    like straw underfoot.

Everyone we wanted to see
was there.

    I almost twisted my ankle in a rut
    that could have once held water.

Your lipstick matched
the red rose and paper flower
bouquet in your hands.

    I followed the rut
    to an outcrop of limestone
    next to a scrub dogwood bush.

A bagpiper played
"She Moves Through the Fair."

    Fiddlehead ferns and lichens
    sprouted among the stones.

There were words spoken,
but they've been forgotten.

                    A pale spring beneath a crust of ice
                    bubbled from a hillside hollow.

You took my arm.

                    I punched through the ice
                    with three fingers.

Your hands were so warm,
a fire in my own.

                    A shiver ran to my elbows
                    as I cupped water to my lips.

There were rings exchanged,
we kissed and began.

                    I have never tasted anything
                    so cold, so pure.

Drift

After the first nine inches, my wife said,
"This snow is absolutely ridiculous," because
we were only talking about the winter storm.

Sprawled on the couch, bodies confined
to woolen boundaries, watching all
the counts go up on the evening news,

we haven't left the neighborhood in fifteen days.
Every night, my dreams are of smoldering,
while mornings are ice, conference calls,

and turning the thermostat up by degrees.
At least we've stopped wearing masks
when we're together, taken to holding

hands, leashes when we venture the dogs
around the block, and always, always,
the slim margins of hope. My fingers a salve

to the small of her back—the spine relaxes, heals.
Anymore, we are too busy in the pandemic
to find lust, so we wrap ourselves in blankets

and wonder how the weather around us turned
frigid. As the world outside goes all white,
we rekindle what it's like to be in love.

Grackle, Grackle

Precursor to summer wind,
chattering palettes
and trembling quarrels,
or on twigs, comatose
as slow cooked beans.

I have always wanted
to admire their plucky flight,
call it "resplendent in apogee,"

but my head begs dust
to stay dust, my head
wants kinder equations
than their collective
designation as "plagues"—

most times I see them
as oily grubbers
picking lint from seed.

God over grackles, tiny subset
that watches over all wings,
makes Spring behind
their tail feathers, sun always
in their stuttered wake.

Maybe the Jay

If you want to change
your life of dull longing,
pay attention
to the blue jay's screech—
almost a directive
to be engaged,
a kind of summons
to another velocity.

You'll know for certain
you are in his space—
the plot of backyard
from stump to fencepost—
by the pitch and grating
of his hailing shriek.

Rise, but bend down,
step forward, but delay,
now glance up
to the high treetops—
bare branches against
the brilliant sun
a conformation of filigree.

If you are lucky,
and chosen, and pure,
you will glimpse him
before he launches
his blue-white contrail
through the summer air.

To caution invaders,
he calls out what he can
and cannot change,
on his way
to survey or defend
this small portion
of the known world
you both share.

Take Flight

—for Jane

Swarming the silver maple's branches
in a loose murmuration of gold pocked rust,
a constellation of starlings chatters
their explanations of divinity
to the wind.
                    To demonstrate, they ascend
to form a consensus midair,
an adulation in no shape other than a cloud,
a blurry mist twisting like salvation
over a green memory of Tennessee hills.

You've been here so long
your name is etched on the stoop,
a house number unrecognizable in faded paint.
Your tired heart has finally forgotten
how to speak its pulse.
                    The past
is the dry field you bless each morning with seed,
adrift you sit and watch the starlings—
their incomprehensible psalms of the body
transfigure into the body they become.

Hex

The cloud drift, silver-
plated overhead,
                obscures
turkey buzzards circling
before their quick
                descent
to a dead rabbit torn
by the fieldside.
                All signs
and portents point
to a summer
                of calm
despair. The rabbit
a dark spot by
                the road's
berm, a broken thing
splayed open
                spilling fate.
Should I read it, like
a witch's spell?
                Its entrails
on closer inspection
form a question.
                Rain?
Rebirth? All things ending?
Tractors churn
                far afield,
horizons to dust.
Another April left

        behind,
I go back inside. The birds
like stones begin
        to drop.

Consoling the Flock

Some lives are torn to the bone
and some are torn apart.
There will be fleece stained
pink with blood, teeth
into the softest throat,
hooves that kick and falter
the eternal and empty
November night air.

Before the bleating
becomes screaming,
and the wild stampeding
turns to terror, there
is little we can ever do
to keep the coyotes at bay.

But there will also be meadows
days from now, some calmer
semblance of normalcy—
sunflower, sweet feed,
alfalfa, and fresh water
straight from the garden hose.

Spring is only months away,
when the fireflies stutter
and the barn finch calls
from the stable's highest rafter.
Repeating, repeating,
the song of the pasture—
in praise of fortitude,
in praise of the meek.

III

Limestone

Bones below that summon us back.
Creek bed appearing overnight after rain—
the field eroded till the stones emerged.
Thick sheep fescue rimming the trench,
and the many eyes peering below the mane.
The sparkling vast periphery of stone.
The Our Father before bed and after sunrise,
before all the glorious chickens pecking.
An ambulance backfiring twice down the road.
Black dirt at the center of the campfire ring.
The song the deaf neighbor girl tries to sing
pedaling her bike in a circle all day.
The bald spots where stones begin to rise,
trees finding no purchase in the field.
The brush and scrap timber piles abandoned.
Oak of kindness, tranquility, and seeking.
The rusted wire fence meandering aimless.
The horse pasture separate from over there
where a ring-necked pheasant takes flight.
The hand on the back at Sunday prayer service.
The uselessness of obsidian, marble, granite.
The periphery and center of all our sadness.
Illegible inscriptions erased by rain.

Condolence

—for Teddy West

What I wanted to say about memory
has already been said then forgotten.
Like archaeology, the dust covers
everything—from buried artifacts,
to books, to the back of my throat—
and leaves me speechless and cowed
with this handful of flowers
I desperately don't want you to see
as a symbol of my disregard.
So here they are: two daisies, a lily,
three clouds of baby's breath
and some trailing stems of nasturtium,
but not the little card I left blank
abandoned on the kitchen counter
next to my favorite empty coffee cup.
Trust me, nothing I could have said
in that tiny space would have mattered,
would have turned back the clock
or set the world where it belongs.
See, already I'm rigging clichés
instead of excavating my memories,
recalling those sun-pocked city streets
we wandered like two explorers
unfettered by any fear of a future
lingering always just out of sight
in the darkened alleyway. I can barely
remember any of it, now that
we've turned the corner. Which is why,
finally, I thought it best to replace

all the words with flowers—sad props
fading light and wilting in my fist—
holding fast to a memory of beauty
for however long we're allowed.

Father at the End

I barely remember him then
(or is it more trying not to)
when he wasn't outsleeping
the neuropathy in his body,
that rundown house he paid for.

Cigarette haze aureoles
his bald head, like a dream
of the kitchen table. I give him
a shot of insulin to his belly
after cheese crackers and milk.

Then his strained rising
to kiss my mother's forehead,
"Goodnight, dear."
While she watches evening mass
drone on Channel 17,

he ambles past the couch
on his way to nowhere
with even less light.
"Can I get you anything, Dad?"
An asthmatic pause

inflates the hallway's dark.
"Yeah, you can get me a son
that won't leave." But I'm
already one foot to the door,
all my things are packed.

And not one month later
after the quick decline
(the doctor's words
not my own), machines
hum like gnostic saints,

a glowing vigil
around his sleeping form.
I squeeze my hand under him
to pull out the bed pan,
spilling piss all over the sheets.

He startles awake, asks,
"What are you doing?"
Now a puddle I'll need to clean.
The hum so loud, antiseptic
singes the back of my throat.

All I'm thinking is what I've given,
what's yet to be taken.
I want to say, "I'm trying
to show how much I love you,"
but instead snap back,

"What does it look like
I'm doing?" already turning
to leave. Barely there
I hear him say from far away,
"I can't open my eyes to see."

Pretense

After losing my shirt, I'm driving home
from the Friday night poker game,
where a colleague told me
how four of his previous friends

died after playing Texas hold'em with him,
all on the highway, drunk going too fast—
this as I was holding three kings and a wild deuce.

So now, I'm thinking about dying,
wondering how much I'm asking for it,
head-on swerve into oncoming traffic
down the narrow two-lane road.

I need to knock on wood, crack
the red eggshell of a smile, three pinches of salt
over my shoulder, just to keep the wheel straight.

But I keep seeing those four faceless dead men
slamming into the gray specter of no tomorrow—
sparks and diamonds of windshield stone,

the junkyard smell of vinyl, stale beer
and gasoline, Jaws of Life extricating
the mess left behind. The more bad thoughts
I think, the safer I feel, drifting into the other lane.

Almost home but I keep passing ghosts,
thumbs in the air of the future tense,
billowing bedsheets by the side of the road.

Even the rumble strips sound like shovelfuls of dirt
rapping on a padded ceiling overhead—
Somebody has to go out first, the last thing
he said, laying a pair of sad jacks on the table.

Passion

Take this guy on my right—
the one questioning the lightbulb
in quick broken Slovak,
calling for another round
from this end of the bar,
finishing off his third
pickled-beet egg,
telling no one who listens
his dreams.
          He waits
at this bar on the corner
of County Road J and US 20
from five to five-thirty
every day. He waits to be taken
home after work, after fifteen
years at the slide-bolt punch,
eight more hours
of the same goddamn thing,
half-hour lunch break
from the slaughterhouse floor—
a single stick of salami—
he waits for one more
shot and cold beer.
          Consider
that he wants none of this. Now
consider his singular desire—
the silver blur of flight— which
you know little about, and which
he'll never reach. And if you
were drinking next to him,

bumping the elbow of his replica
bomber jacket—the golden wings,
fake patches and medals,
the name of a squadron
that never left the ground—
you might call it passion,
and you'd sit down beside him
and wait, and wait
for the rest of your life.

Country Dark

Half-drunk at The Roadhouse, I asked the bartender
missing the index finger on her left hand
if she still felt it when she went to scratch her ear
or poke inside her nostril. She told me, "Only
when I need it the most."
                        At first, I thought
she was asking to borrow money, so I paid
for my whiskey and slipped out the side door
next to the men's room, into the freezing parking lot
parallel to Ten-Mile Creek.
                        Walking to my car, I saw
the full moon on the water, a perfect roundness
like the single dime I'd left for her tip,
bright as a headlight, and I suddenly understood
everything she didn't say.
                        What must it be like
to need the one thing you can't have?
It could be as simple as a finger to pick your nose
or a December moon staring back at you
from deeper water somehow not yet frozen.
                        It leaves
a watermark, a blurred shadow in the wavering light,
another ghost where I thought home resided—
memory closing the door on the past tense
where all things go, then go missing.

The Five Hearts of Texas

   I.
Rustic, the way wind
swaggers this prairie,
timothy grass
as a sort of transcendence.
And by grass, I mean
golden fires,
blasted sun
over frayed copper wire,
bugs and linnets,
emerald grasshoppers
swarming,
the glass shells
of every eternal humming thing.

   II.
On the sixth day
the armadillo grew
into his shell, took off
his wings for good.

He settled here
because the weather
made a promise
to his claws—
armadillo hands,
newly formed stigmata.

We gave him a name,
little armored one, and stones

the very idea
of being armadillo.

   III.
I do not speak Spanish,
                 so I didn't know
what the man in line
at the post office wanted.
The only two words
I recognized
were *Texas* and *sea*.
I walked away from him
like I disappear
              from the blind,
unrecognizable.
I thought he meant
the Gulf of Mexico
instead of saying yes
to Texas.

   IV.
Pieces of spaceship
fell from the sky,

and some people
took them home
and some tried
to sell them
on eBay
claiming private
property, claiming
they didn't know

what they had,
didn't know that

pieces of spaceship
fell from the sky.

And seven astronauts
were incinerated.
We said heroes,
we said brave,
the first sign
like a comet
returning,
a precursor,
a prophecy, the beginning
of another age where

pieces of spaceship
began falling from the sky.

 V.
In the dream of Texas
  my father
raised the baby goat.
  A cereal bowl
of river water
  held to its bottom lip.

I was six years old
  we were soaked
on our way home
  from fishing
the creek bed

        where my grandfather
held his heart
        and became a stone.

We stopped—
        the baby goat,
my father, the stone, and I—
        to teach me
to tie my shoes
        with one hand,
to walk for miles
        through the dust
without ever
        being recognized.

Desperados

By the seventh day we were so thirsty
we shot the last of the stolen horses
with our last two bullets, drank their blood
just to keep our tongues from turning
to worn boot soles, straw and sandstone.
Pappy fixed his specialty—horse ribs fried
in bacon grease. We ate like men condemned
beneath the eyes of the known and dead
constellations, the coyote's mournful riff
ringing between arroyos, a scrub brush fire
dwindling out. Our biggest problem was
the law, with its tin insistence of wrong,
more bullets and rested reinforcements
less than a day's ride away. Always another
small town, another swagger waiting to drop,
the post office smell of old paper money.
For once I agreed with Red: what we needed
was a quiet bunk to settle down on, a hole
in the wall behind the wall. But out here
there are only bad men, lost and dead horses,
and no way but with blood to go underground.

Xiuhtecuhtli

—the Aztec God of Time

There is another revealing
in the gaze of the pig
every morning watching you
from behind the rusted hog panels,
chewing the thick gauge wires
with mealy yellow teeth
as you try reaching for the feed pan,
its daily offering of grain.
                        It's the gaze
of the drunk at the bus stop on Locust
your second year at college, shirtless,
a scar from ear to armpit,
who couldn't stop coughing,
who held your eyes with his eyes,
doubled over, dropped to his knees,
a dead bird splayed-out
on the ground before him,
his spittle sprinkling the sidewalk
in flecks of blood.
                        Walking home
that night, the back alley ending
at your door, you couldn't stop thinking
about those eyes, their utter lack
of concern, the thousand-mile stare
that seemed to be asking—*where to now?*—
the same question you asked yourself
every time you walked that path,
                              as every time

the pig gets in your way, or snorts
and pants its grin, wiping its face
in something rotten on the ground.
When you were twenty, the cigarettes
burned one into the next, and
the walk home from class was dark
and cold as the cheap ½ pint of vodka
waiting on your freezer shelf—
stepping backwards was something
you practiced no matter the time of year,
a litany of tomorrows you thought
might never end.
                Is that
what you were expecting?
That time would turn in on itself
like an eternal figure-eight,
that the bottle might never empty,
that the dull electric bassline
droning from the bedroom
where someone was doing another line
might play loud enough to keep you
from every assignment past due
the next morning? The dead sparrow
always in the gutter where you left it—
right there with the drunk
and his stage IV cancer.
                        But look at you now,
forty years later, picturing
the shape of time as a ziggurat,
where climbing each level
pulls the thinning atmosphere
from your lungs, till one day
you'll reach the narrowed top—as far

as you can go. Then, stepping
from the shower wrapped in a towel,
or just rising from a straight back chair,
the last light you'll see
will burn the brightest you've ever known
till something else
takes over in a fiery ring of glory,
or nothing else.
                             It's just you
and the pig now, his insatiable hunger
and those eyes buried beneath
the four folds of his brow, coarse black hair
covering every inch of his head,
sitting there like some fat god
taking you back to places
you never thought you'd return, asking,
Where to now? all over again.
                                     He'll need
fresh water and a full bowl of food,
and the hay that makes up his bed
needs to be raked and cleaned up
before morning can pass into what may
be your last pleasant afternoon.
Before he'll consider you
no longer a threat to anything,
you'll need to be still and bow down,
break your gaze from the past
and its burden of burnt offerings.
Only then will he stop chewing the wires
and finally get out of your way.

A Decent God

I'd like to find just one
who understands the cost
of hallowed mornings spent
neck bent in hushed prayer
before the early mass begins;
who listens without wrath,
or judgment, or contempt,
as the seconds tick away
like stars disintegrating
in the uneventful waking light.

The voices in the old stories
always asked what more
they could do after the penance,
the lesson spelled in stone
carried down from high places—
don't kill—which in its own way
was a kind of gentle decency.

Don't get me wrong, I am
grateful for this tattered map
folded in my hands, the stars,
though temporary, overhead,
another season's harvest and chaff
winnowing away memory
like oak shavings planed
from this rough board of days.
But the granite blocks mortared
in hollow semblances of faith

down the road from my farm
echo with a sadness when I enter.

Everywhere I turn I am witness
to regret, or worse, guilt,
in each congregant's glare. It's not
for me to decide who deserves
salvation—leave that for the field
and its mouth and eye sockets
filling with shovelfuls of wet clay.
There's nowhere left for me to go
with this burden of prayers,
bundle of hours become years,
no singing voice born
for useless hymns of glory be.

The Penitent

The church choir sings hosanna somewhere
seven miles north. Before the sun even rises,
the widower is driving to the cemetery,
a shovel in the bed of his pickup truck.
He holds the wheel with just two fingers
fishtailing broken asphalt and patchy ice.
All along 64, roadside crosses, dirty white
plastic flowers, dirty white wooden posts,
remnants of winter wheat beat down by rain.
The farmhouse up the road burned down
last week, no one knows where the family went.
The reservoir, another echo chamber in blue,
spills its stony banks, the same way sleep
inundates and returns him here. Now
the knees of his pants harden with mud.
Now the church doors rattle and open.
What would you have me do with all this?
the field sparrow asks. I feed it anyway,
picking myself up from the breathing
sodden ground. I too could take a shovel to it
but the frostline quells and refuses to recede.

Guardian of the Farm

In this moment, in the violence
of all this world we inhabit—
the crushed shell of the duck egg
next to the nest, the hutch door
pried open, the drake still beating
his furious wings at the tracks
trailing into high clover, storms
to the south dragging cloud vapors
like misty veils through the lower sky—
it's too easy to forget forgiveness
and go fetch my gun, because I am
American, rural, Midwestern,
and revenge is a favored disciple,
full of bluster and no second chance.
But when I see it, the muskrat,
in its bedraggled coat, slick fur
more knotted tassel than quill,
clay black eyes the shade of mud,
yolk dried yellow trailed down its chin,
rising on hind legs in the back field,
all judgment is temporarily repaired
by wonder. Had the dog done the same
his punishment would be meager.
But thunder roils the sky and shakes
the poplars, and I'm raising the barrel
half-hearted to convince myself
I have this one job to become.

Field Guide

    I. Goldenrod

For two weeks every year I'm alive
They rise and burn the meadow
        Amber shock and cacophony
        Ceding to wonder

In the field's sway a thousand blooms
Balance a horizon on its brow
        Glory and tiny humming things
        Are the world in all directions

Florets smolder on for days
Casually ignite each afternoon
        Like goldfinch bellies streaking by
        Brief blessings however glimpsed

September's end and the landscape wearies
The weight of each blossom's crown
        Tattered skirts and hollow stems
        A rattle of shin bones in wind

    II. Bull Thistle

Nights the moon
buries itself
under blankets
of spite and cloud cover,
subtracting hours

from your life
like spent money
taxed and overdrawn,
friends gone
or going into the fog,
empty pockets,
the torn heel
of the rain boot,
so many holes
in the garden soil
where lilac bushes
once instructed air
to bloom,
and the howling,
twilight into morning,
diminished by hunger,
rising off the field
like a recitative,
then resolving
over the bull thistle,
the bruised or vacant
heart which you will
never come to accept
in the same way
the earth has,
prickly seedhead,
noxious thorny stalk,
lateral roots
through stocky clay
which refuse to budge
no matter the pulling
or digging,

the burning or cutting,
which must grow
to the center
of all things
bound and binding
in a knot.

III. Wild Phlox

You've brought the burdens
you paid for,
carried them this far.

Laments and confessions
from childhood,
obligations...

For their part,
there is no judgment,
no recompense,

tasked to chiefly spread
by the willowed creek-side.
All this time

the weight of your life
condensing like water,
looking for a cloud

of black-eyed blossoms,
flurry of bee buzz
a roadside pause.

What would you name
a grief so purple
it singes your eyes?

    IV. Curly Dock

To tower above the field
is to know the secret
of wind's final plan.
Everything swept clean—
dust, choked air,
all else bent down or lifted
in a vanquishing torrent.

To raise a fruiting stem
in celebration, bitter harvest
of brown seed, is another
way of standing tall
even while you're bending.

Another staff shaken
to the sky in defiance,
hairless leaves clasping
like hands below,
in faith the glorious rains
will follow to finish
the task the wind began.

    V. Milkweed

How can I be sure
    this time

you are
among the pods
and not
    like last time
in the voices
below the nave
    I am only
    the spiked burst
    pink blossomed
        sweet mercy
    months gone
    cocooned
        downy seed
    waiting to disperse
All around
the monarchs
    wings carry me
translucent
to cathedral glass
blood/wine
    luminosity
wrapped in wire
    And whatever
    drew me
        away from there
    drew me
    without portents
    anointed palms
        a milky sap
    an empty heart
I am speaking
to you now

      as if nothing
came between us
but the wind
      at my back
I may as well
go on talking

      to the field

Hollow

In the meadow there is this green undoing,
this diastolic thumping,
this deference to cloud-light,
milkweed floss,
and the torn, red-tipped wing of blackbird
rendered by hawk-strike,
all becoming equal parts
suffering into resignation,
maybe faith.
          I have nowhere else
to go with my shovel
but out here, into the past
making holes.
          Sanctuary
is not what I would call it—
the goldenrod has gone
to umber dry stems, bones fill the earth,
it bends and swallows,
but a single startled sunray
shimmers the back of the rabbit
darting from a swale
of orchard grass, follows it into the ground.

Ending

Pity the patter
         of rain
in the abandoned field
of mud,
      cornstalk stubble
broken finger bones,
rows
    of repentance,
the tracks of a wounded
doe,
    harbinger of storm
of all-too-common
sorrow.
      Pity the field
picked over
        by crows,
oily shadows' murk,
windbreak
      of bare oak,
the bone and fossil
the beaks become,
          shovel
and chisel,
      roadside blot
passing fallow acres
flat line,
    horizons dull.
And pity
      the sequence
of ceaseless tractors tilling

the fields,
        glyphosate, seed
and gasoline spill,
            diesel
drenching roadside
culverts, harvest,
           cull,
furrow, plough, sow,
repeat, repeat.
        Harvests
slough topsoil to sand,
to blight.
        Although
tomorrow
     the sun,
or not the sun but
the utter
     lack of clouds,
may make the sky seem
brilliant
     born again
the field is drowning.
Pity
   for all the ground
is and is
     becoming.

The Center

—for my wife

The center of the field
is the point below
the highest crest
in the winter cloud cover.
The point of the field
is to believe it goes on
forever without us.
From this perspective
the whole sky is swooning,
and nothing grows
but the dark of dusk.

I'm on my tractor
turning compost
in the wooden bin,
at its own center
between the barn
and the barren garden.
I'm moving just to keep
warm before the new year
smothers the old
in a frigid wind
that smells like my sweat.
My hands, clutched
on the wheel, ache,
and a damp scarf
over my nose because

you tied the knot
tight behind my neck.

One of the goats
I care for like our child
is crossing the field slow
in her silky white coat.
From this distance
she looks like the absence
of the tall dead grass,
a cigarette burn
in filmstock, a synapse
of snow. She looks
after herself, now
able to find her way
back to the barn
without a lead
around her neck,
she cries and bleats
even when there's no one
there to listen.

Finished, I park
by a pine stump and glance
back to the house,
where you watch
from the porch window,
inside, warm. We are
moving farther away
from the summer
of little rain, slim harvest
of corn and broccoli
browning on the stalk,

the past a reel
unwound, still spinning.
Next year, we plan
to move the boundaries
of the field, to make
room for pumpkins,
watermelon and squash,
though what we call
boundaries are arbitrary
as tilled earth.
Will the center
remain the same?

I want to get out
of this cold, to you
and the fire that's been
burning since before
the kindling set,
dinner the stone
of potato in a bowl,
breath no longer visible
in the air before me.

But there are chores—
brush to pile, animals
that must eat, many eggs
to gather—and always
plans to make for
tomorrow and the next
after that. I can't wait
to make them with you.
The field remains
unresolved before me

below the overcast sky,
but I keep moving closer,
from ordained beginning
to imagined end,
across the space we are
making between.

Acknowledgments

Grateful acknowledgment is made to the following journals in which some of the poems in this collection first appeared:

After Happy Hour Review: "Hex," "Xiuhtecuhtli"
Amethyst Review: "Hollow"
Anacapa Review: "Consoling the Flock," "Limestone"
Anti-Heroin Chic: "Binomial"
Cathexis Northwest Press: "The Five Hearts of Texas," "Stump"
Chautauqua: "After All"
I-70 Review: "Drift," "Pretense"
Lake Effect: "The Penitent"
Last Stanza Poetry Journal: "The Hidden Spring"
The Mill: "Field Guide, Part V. Milkweed"
New Note Poetry: "Smoke"
Plainsongs: "Certainty"
Plants and Poetry Journal: "If a Tree Falls"
Poetry South: "Grackle, Grackle," "Take Flight"
Radar: "The Center"
SALT: "Azaleas," "Condolence," "Retreat"
Slant: "Night Lights"
South Florida Poetry Review: "Passion"
Split Rock Review: "Maybe Mice"
Stoneboat Literary Journal: "Orbits"
Tar River Poetry: "Overcast
Trace Fossils Review: "Guardian of the Farm"

Two Review: "Desperados"
Wild Roof Journal: "Animals in the Dark"

"Certainty," "Consoling the Flock," "If a Tree Falls," "Maybe Mice," "Retreat," and "Thanksgiving" appeared in *Holler*, a letterpress limited-edition chapbook (APoGee Press, 2021).

"Winter Follows" appeared as a letterpress keepsake for the 5 Poets 5 Parks Celebration sponsored by Metroparks Toledo (Pineapple Press, 2024).

Grateful acknowledgment also to the Sundress Academy for the Arts for a 2019 Writer's Residency, the Rockvale Writer's Colony for a 2023 Residency, and the Arts Commission of Greater Toledo for a 2020 Merit Award, made possible through the support of ProMedica, the Ohio Arts Council, and the National Endowment for the Arts.

About the Author

Timothy Geiger is the author of three previous full-length poetry collections: *Weatherbox*, winner of the 2019 Vern Rutsala Poetry Prize from Cloudbank Books; *The Curse of Pheromones* (Main Street Rag); and *Blue Light Factory* (Spoon River Poetry Press). He is also the author of ten chapbooks, most recently *Holler* (APoGee Press). His poems have been included in the anthologies *American Poetry: Next Generation* (Carnegie Mellon University Press), *Place of Passage* (Storyline Press), and *A Fine Excess: Contemporary Writers at Play* (Sarabande Books). His honors include a Pushcart Prize XVII; a Holt, Rinehart and Winston Award in Literature; and many state and local grants from Alabama, Minnesota, and Ohio. He is the proprietor of Aureole Press, a letter-press imprint producing chapbooks of contemporary poetry at the University of Toledo, where he teaches creative writing, poetry, and book arts. He lives on a small farm in Swanton, Ohio, with his wife and all their animals.

www.ingramcontent.com/pod-product-compliance
Lightning Source LLC
Chambersburg PA
CBHW060532080526
44586CB00012B/708